THE BOOK

OF ANGELS

New and selected poems

2000—2025

The Book of Angels

New and Selected Poems
2000-2025

Lyndon Walker

Cover : Antonio Cavallucci, **Head of an Angel**, (Italy, 1752 – 1795). Los Angeles County Museum of Art. Used with permission. Author Photos: Red Background by Michael Gray Griffith and Abbey Road by Jane Refshauge. Back cover: Lyndon Walker.

ISBN 9781764120012

Walleah Press
South Launceston
Tasmania, Australia 7249
www.walleahpress.com.au
ralph.wessman@walleahpress.com.au

THE BOOK

OF ANGELS

New and Selected

Poems 2000—2025

LYNDON WALKER

'Behind every beautiful thing there's been some kind of pain'
~ Bob Dylan
"It's Not Dark Yet, But It's Gettin' There"

'The single biggest problem in communication is the illusion that it
has taken place.'
~ George Bernard Shaw.

'Beware of falling angels': Sign outside the Santa Maria della
Salute Church in Venice in the early 1970's, during the resto-
ration of its marble angels

Contents

About The Author 86

Notes 87

ALSO BY LYNDON WALKER

POETRY

P C (Tomato Press, Stanmore, 1974)

Adam Scolds – with Graham Rowlands and Graeme Pitt
(Cochon, Townsville. 1976)

The Green Wheelbarrow (Makar Press, University of
Queensland, St Lucia, 1976)

Singers and Winners (Pariah Press, Kew, 1984)

So Many Rivers, So Much To Learn
(Five Islands Press, Wollongong, 1st edition, 2000,
University of Melbourne, 2nd edition, 2015)

SHORT STORIES
Because I Made Her Happy I Said (People's Library, Hobart. 2018)

ACKNOWLEDGEMENTS

Grateful acknowledgement is made to the following journals and anthologies where many of these poems have previously appeared:

Meanjin, Overland, The Canberra Times, The Age, Going Down Swinging, Five Poetry Journal, Australia New Zealand Journal of Family Therapy, The Blue Giraffe, Leaves Literary Journal, The Medical Journal of Australia, A Sudden Presence: Poetry from the Inaugural ACU Literature Prize 2013, Walking the Dogs: The Pariah Press Anthology 1994, Earth Against Heaven: A Tiananmen Square Anthology, Off The Record, Aspect: Art and Literature, Poet's Choice, North of Capricorn: An Anthology of Verse, the Montreal International Poetry Prize (published online); and most recently in *Love: The ACU Poetry Prize 2023 Anthology.*

Poems in this *New and Selected* have also appeared in my previous collections:
The Green Wheelbarrow (1976), *Singers and Winners* (1984), and *So Many Rivers, So Much To Learn* (2000; 2015).

Awards for poems from this collection include:
First Prize, The Sunshine Coast Short Story and Poetry Prize; First Prize, Pablo Neruda Poetry Prize; Longlisted, The Montreal International Poetry Prize; and Shortlisted, ACU International Poetry Prize, 2013, 2019 and 2023.

I would also like to express my gratitude to those who have supported my writing process over the years. To Alex Skovron for reading the initial manuscript and for suggesting this be a New & Selected collection. To Jennifer Comptom's Carrum writing group, especially Michelle Leber, Garth Madsen, Susan Fealy and others who attended at various times. To Robert Adamson, who read my manuscript and offered support and encouragement.

Acknowledgement is also made to Monique Sereda, who supported my writing when I first came to Tasmania and to the Poetry group who meet every month at the Royal Hotel in Brisbane Street: Marilyn, Carol, Wendy, Yvonne, Mark, Graeme, Anne, Tim and others.

I greatly appeciate the efforts over years in a mutual exchange and support of our writing between Gayelene Carbis and myself. She has kept my spirits up when the writing world has sometimes been arbitrary and whimsical and did an extraordinary job in proof reading this manuscript and suggesting changes. Thank you Gayelene.

READERS' RESPONSES TO WALKER'S WORK

Whatever "it" is, Walker has it
— THOMAS SHAPCOTT

The Book of Angels
Heartbreaking
— STEVE BIDDULPH

Stunning
— WILLO DRUMMOND

So Many Rivers, So Much to Learn:
It has been worth the long wait for Lyndon Walker's new collection of poetry. These poems have the savour of a hard-won sardonic wisdom. But there is also a subtle lyrical intimacy that can wind around the reader like a protective charm.
— DOROTHY PORTER

For Jean
Who cared for me when I lost my leg ; 2021 - 2024

ANGELS IN THE AFTERNOON

Morning

The light comes into the room. The light enters the room.
    The light steals
Into the room slowly, like a thief. And what does it steal?
    It stealeth away darkness.

It stealeth away night. It stealeth away the sins of the world.
    It stealeth away
Our knowledge of darkness, or rather it adds itself
    to nothingness gradually

So as to reveal itself to us and at the same time to reveal
    the world in all its glory
An' its television an' its grace.

Now we must be more modern. We must be more scientific.
    We must say light from the star
Thousands of light years away has somehow entered the room
    exhausted
From its travels in straight or curving lines through space
    and time and rested gently
On the atoms of things and joined them in the trick and gift of
    gradual solidity.

The light has entered our own consciousness
    in just the same way it would have
Entered the eyes and nerve cells of Alexander the Great or
    Joan of Arc or Christ
    or Buddha or Allah
Or Salman Rushdie – Light you see like God Herself
    like God Himself
Does not discriminate. For we are like lizards if we are alive
    to receive it

Light will enter through our eyelids even while they are shut
          and we are essentially
To all intents and purposes sleeping.

It will sit down in an armchair in the room and begin
          a conversation in our brain
The tiniest amount will excite and elicit the production of
          serotonin so that not only
Will we begin to experience light and the day and the world
          again but we will feel
Good about doing so.

Now, just only for me the light like an excellent slow and
          deliberate painter
Has gently begun to colour the room and for me the world in
          the first and subtlest
Shades of black and then blue
          and then the differentiation of shapes
The darkening forming coming into being of the square heavy
          don't-hit-your-shin-on-this-it-will-hurt chest of drawers
On the different coloured
          but not yet different
Coloured but only different shapes of clothing
          has only the soft honey effect
Of matching the flowing presence of my warm lover's body
          and my own here in the
Big bed in the magic of newdayness and a simplicity which
          matches the complex
Nuclear reactions in the sun our own star and the gradual
          learning of childhood

I have taken the great light of the world
          from Christina's shoulders
Christina in the painting by Andrew Wyeth.
          Christina who is blind.
And placed it on the side of the distant barn.

ANGELS IN THE AFTERNOON

Jean says the sun has made a hole for itself in the sky.
A brown dove is sitting in that tree.
Birds don't need houses or possessions
A branch is their furniture.

I'm too old not to see
Perfection in everything
The leaves turning golden to brown in Autumn
And the deepest green in Spring.

Today in Beauty Point
The actual name of the place where I live
The clouds have come down to settle
On the land and the water
As if to tell us we are in heaven already.

I want to write a story
About a man who read all the texts
Of the world's major religions
But didn't notice he was living
With an angel in his house.

When we approach the café
The rain becomes heavier
But when we park
The rain stops altogether.
Angels are protected from the weather.

Night brings a little light rain on the roof
The sound of angels dancing.

THE HUM OF THE WORLD

Sometimes the world hums.
The warm good food in your stomach hums.
The good people who cooked it are humming
In the kitchen.
The live chatter from the people at other
Tables
And even the annoying children
Hum.

The knowledge that today at work
Where sometimes everything can go wrong
Or just a little out of whack
Or mediocre
Or just so so
Today
Went so right
Sits in your happy head
And hums.

And the relationship that sometimes takes so
Much work
Tonight
Takes a night off
And walks on the beach
In the warm evening air
Humming at the moon.

Every mad bad and crazy thing
Has fallen asleep at the devil's table
And the angels of all that's good
Crank up the world's great turbine
While neighbourhood dogs

And couples out for a stroll
Waiting for the lights
On a street corner
Lift their heads
Ever so slightly
And listen carefully
To the faint hum of the world

COASTAL MUSIC

I. APOLLO BAY

The ocean was with us all night
Thunderous and heavy
Rolling over in its sleep
And further out, deep
Full of whales and coldness.

Your tiny sounds as you slept
My creeping through the house so as not to wake you
To write this.
Outside
Barely breathing
The dark, unwoken world.

II. HER SOCKS

I knew they were her socks when I picked them up
And put them with other things
Into my bag. Two small socks without dislike or suspicion.

She had thrown them off, quickly
To race out across the road
To tell the man
Whose hat had blown off
Where he could find it.
She's like that

And when she came back
Laughing and breathless
The huge blue sky her whole canvas
The wind blowing hair across her face
Leaping at me
Like a silver fish from a stream of pure joy
I lifted the camera I had been playing with
And gave thanks.

III. BECAUSE YOU ARE MUSIC

Because you are music
I drive carefully
Up the mountain road through forest
And patches of light
Into your absence.

JOUISSANCE: **THE TRAIN TO PAIN & JOY**

After Svetozar Piletić: DVERI (The Double Doors) translated by Nada Lane
For my daughter, Johanna

On a day when the sun was landing on the platform like a plane
I was waiting for the Airtrain to Brisbane Airport
And I noticed all the other passengers were carrying their luggage
        of pain
But they were still standing

I kept looking for those rare and beautiful people
Who openly carry their luggage of joy
But it was a Sunday, and a slow day
And I saw no one of that description until we
Went to sit on the other side of the platform
Out of the sun and I saw you
And when the train pulled in
(twenty minutes late and we missed our plane)
I looked in the reflecting windows of the train and I saw me too

And then I remembered when the baby was born
And I realised
That sometimes life is given to us
Just like that
But then sometimes it is harder to carry our luggage of joy than
        our luggage of pain
And it has taken me twenty-three years
To drag my luggage of joy
Onto the platform of this poem

FUNDAMENTAL ATTRIBUTION ERROR

There are fundamental attribution errors we humans make
But the one I hate to teach is called: "Belief in a Just World."

This is not a poem of exactitude.
It is a dream meant to be dreamt.
It is written on a blinding summer day in Melbourne
While it is equally blinding winter in London.

You ask me about Sylvia Plath's poetry
And I tell you I think it's about power and control
Tulips behind bars like caged animals
The absolute attempt to control
Life's unpredictable emotional events
Through the meticulous articulation
Of each experience
About how she became an expert at it
But the attempt inevitably failed.

And as I tell you
I can feel resistance
Rising up
Like a little horse in your chest.

I think she thought her heart
Opening and closing like a tulip
Loved her.
But if you're in England
In December at 5.40am
And you take a tulip from the vase
In the warm house
Into the hard black night, turning into
Cold blue day

And you lie it on the blue snow
And watch as the white wind blows
-              don't be a coward now
-              watch for hours
you will know how wrong she was

NOW YOU ARE GONE

The ice-cream sticks to the roof of my mouth
The nutty ice-cream, little flakes of almond
Or pecan or macadamia, you see
Even when you are gone these little flakes of happiness
Can occur to me

But I can not enjoy them to the full, perhaps
I will leave them in my will
To my beautiful daughter
Like a surprise
And one day
She will wake to find little flakes
Of nutty ice-cream
Like a snowstorm in her mouth.

MY EYES GO OUT LIKE A CRY

(Title from a line by Anne Carson)

You had snuffed me out of your life
Like a candle and my smoke
Had drifted across the high blue landscape of the valley
Of Sienna

All of my poems
Gathered here together
A white flock here on the green hillside
But without a mother

My eyes go out like a cry
You had promised that afternoon
When the sun had his argument with clouds
You did not know you had promised
And now you would deny it
But you had

And now with the soft rain falling
The bells
Before the orchestra
Are crying on the red scarf of memory
I take your hand as if I could
But you have dissolved

And this is the longest, longest, longest
Longest
Image   Your mouth opening   The answer

THE LIMINAL TIME

Memory asks me these questions
Blowing in through the yellow light of dusk
With flies on the restaurant
Veranda. I wonder
As my eyes open over the grey cliché
As cloud kilometres long
Lays itself along the hills
Blowing in through the yellow light of dusk.

I wonder who he is, this man you love
Who the loving of stops you from loving
As my eyes open over the grey cliché
Driving the highway
Murderous to moths
And any idea I might have
Of loving lays itself along the hills
Coming home with you
Blowing in through the yellow light of dusk.

Memory asks me these questions. Your child
Waits. I wait. *Oh sister let's go down*
He waits but might go on unconscious
Like most. As you wait so as it becomes the thing itself
You do. *Oh brothers let's go down*
The weight of
The words in our hands[i]
I ask these questions of memory
Blowing in through the yellow light of dusk.

SHE SAW HOW THE CLOUDS' RAGGED EDGES TOOK LIGHT FROM THE SUN

(Title from a line by Anne Carson)
For Alex

This is not a prayer
To any god who might or might not exist.
This is a prayer
To the bare, damp, rich earth of my country
Stretching as it does
Out of the almost solid
Blue-grey sea throwing itself somewhat hysterically
Onto the rocks like an opera
That seems to understand me
Travelling like some bird
Or thought or plane
Swiftly low across
Sea and sky
Then suddenly the cliffs
Like a rich and complex cake
Cut into. The seemingly endless
Colours of earth in a subtle
And changing palette
Strewn with the magical numbers of latitude
And longitude
And the endless host of characters
Most gathered
Close to the edge and then thinning
Out like a graph towards the centre
This is a nod to the original inhabitants
And to a friend
Who holds some tradition for the children
The Passover stories, Elijah
Or Christ visiting the open door

The full and trembling glass of wine
The Friday night meal all this flown over
Like a spirit visiting each house
The trembling expectant children, and you
Where are you in all this?
I have taken as you have taken me along on all this
Flown across the country
Flown over this swift, over the sea and the coast and the country
and the towns
And the people from this day into the night
Into questions and answers exhausted now
Over the houses
Flown
Like a bird into my heart.

WHO IS IN ME LIKE A BELL?

(Title from a line by Anne Carson)
After Arvo Pärt: Cantus in memoriam Benjamin Britten – for string
orchestra and bell)

After your car has left the car park
Its red lights winking in the dark
Like a bell in the soft air of a clear day
You come ringing into me
As stringent as lemon
In my mouth, the memory
Of your legs in black stockings
As we came from a day
Stuffed full of the best nourishment, poetry
And the most natural of food.

When the train came in the station
It had two lights on behind
The blue light was my baby
The red light was my mind.

But you are so right
It is me who after coming home to you
Could not get used to
Not coming home to you
The lake black and a little ruffled
With white under the full moon
Like a painting, your little dinner of scallops
In the Westin Hotel
Here is joy
In a handful of notes

Your privacy
And my book tucked
Into a stuffed computer bag
Rain on the window
Our short time
Rain on the window
Your baggage
That I carry
For such
A short time

FIRST TIME IN MY LIFE

First time in my life
I've looked out a window and seen the snow falling
Falling into my working day I mean
Falling into my life
As opposed to the times I've gone looking for it
Seen it on the news
Got in the car all rugged up
And gone searching
Like a small holiday.

This time I'd simply risen and showered
In the warm house we'd shared together
As if everything was normal
Driven to the work we'd shared together
As if everything was OK
As if everything would go on
Being this way
As opposed to the distance that is now between us.

I hope the boy you found and loved
Still loves you. I hope the fire you had
In your heart still burns for you
When you want it to
Not when you don't, like it did
Between us two. I hope
One day you may look out the window
And see the snow falling and think of me
Without rancour, without bitterness
Without regret. With only the knowledge
Of that cold place we left
And the clean snow falling.

IMAGES ON HOLIDAY

'There has been no record of a failing of the light
during the thirty years in which it was in my charge'
– Henry Bates Ford, Lighthouse Keeper, Cape Otway, Victoria, 1848 – 1878

The carpet of purple flowers
First trumpet their little martyrdoms
Across the wet concrete of summer
Before small steam makes a magic of the footpath.

Later in Apollo Bay
The God of beauty in men
Seems to have won the lighting tender with the local council.
Light from the new poled spots
Reflects the orange and white and red dinghies
On dark-blue water – the colour of my car
Chopping these colours up together
Like an impressionist late at night
The colour of a cooling breeze
Late at night. A modern film would find the film
Of oil on the foreheads of a people
A loose grouping of people
Walking through this paradise
Because that's what you do in Paradise
Late in the evening, go fishing with your family
Your girlfriend, your dog
As if there were no trouble in the world
And which of us can say
That in our charge
In the whole of a working life
There has been no record
Of a failing of the light.

STORYVILLE

Notes for a poem on New Orleans & Jazz

New Orleans
You got trams like Melbourne
You got
Jazz like New Orleans
You got Jelly Roll
You got 4 bar then more
You got
Buddy Bolden
(his mumma scared)
You got
Spanish tinge
You got
Erotic motion

You got Jelly's great grandmother
You tell a
You the night watchman
You the night watch all right man
You got singin'
You got the piano
You got the Jelly Roll Blues

You got ravi music
You got Storyville
You got Jasmine
So sweet in the air it send you crazy
You call it jazz
You got film an speeded up motion
You got heat
An high emotion

You got Sidney Bechet
The poet of New Orleans music
Creole music
At 16 you leave school
An bring your personality
To your instrument
You love the lonesome blues
Through your horn
You find notes no-one
Even suspected were in that thing

You got the Victor Victrola
1901
No-one thinks of recording Jazz

After Buddy
You have Freddy Keppler
Laughing through the wah-wah mute
In 1914
The Original Creole Orchestra
Hits LA
An buses to Chicago
He very big an very strong
Your mute fly out yo' trumpet onto the dance floor
It in the papers
It never
Happen before

You frightened other people steal your stuff
February 26th 1917
The Original Dixieland Orchestra
5 white musicians

Led by Nick
La Rocca
Play Dixieland One Step
You play
Horses
You play
Roosters
You play
Around on record
First time in history
250,000 copies at 50 cents each

Then you got influenza
You got nervous breakdown
You got construction – no-one ever know
You play music
You got
Buddy locked up in the Jacksonville
Insane Asylum
His mumma
Get so scared she call police
He never play the horn again
You got
T' excuse me right now
I got ta
Get some sleep
You know what I mean?

LARGE INTERIOR IN RED: MATISSE

Kitsch red Swedish modernity
As functional and expendable
As throw-away swabs
In an operating theatre
It casually meets itself
And introduces us coolly
To the new etiquette

This is nearly the twenty-first century
And we no longer recognise
Our friends so easily. Wasn't he
In Vietnam? Weren't we
At school together? I now manage a hospital
And that girl at the table in the Black Cat Cafe
Playing with her cutlery as if
They were surgical implements, wasn't she
The first one in that tiny room as students
Fascinated with the little lake of blood?

Now she doesn't know you, or at least gives no sign
You watch the shimmer of veins
Just under the eyelid's skin
And embarrassed
Turn the colour of the painting.

This is the new nonchalance. It is just like
A waiting room
The colour of an extraction. All who view it
Are synonymous with catalogues.
Watch the small red dots appear
In front of your pale faces.

Take off your dark cold coats. Warm yourselves
At its glow. It is as flat
And red
As an accident.

SINCE I DID PLANT THE MOON

It's a time for harvesting the sea
Planting out my heart with hope
In all the days and nights ahead
That I might work and sleep beside
My many loves and shared
And all but gone too soon
And following those thousand roads
That watched the months and skies all change
Since I did plant the moon

TUESDAY MORNING IN ITHACA

I like the way the blue streaked walls
In Santucci's silhouettes the mother's
White hoodie and the child's grey top.

Their hands are both to their mouths
And that tells us there are things suppressed

As if the ancient pottery mask
Between them on the wall from its Mediterranean
Home in myth says it all. Ulysses is sailing

Somewhere in the world. The wife and child are waiting
Here while time stalls for them awhile
Asleep on their island of coffee.

TEXT THIS!

The sun coming up over the grey sea
Under clouds so early
You can smell that sea in the breeze
That moves the light down on your cheek and arm.

A girl's eyes with nothing but love
So close to your face that you know
Why poets have used the word 'swimming.'

The drive down through forest
Or along Great Ocean Road with tree smell
Blowing in the open windows, these tyres
Love the road.

The pale legs getting off the bus
That your whole body wanted to follow
Instead of a day's work in the factory.

The looping dive of skinny tanned androgyny
Clear water splashing the dark speckle
Of rocks near the top of the mountain
And the falls above the town.

Pebble's fifth birthday at the Taj Mahal
And the guarded happy women
Guiding her through now.

Sitting alone in a cafe in the southern city
With all your loves across the unforgiving
Spread of country and open colours
Of the world on a map of childhood.

Knowing everything that comes to you
In one moment. See if you can find the words
And text that.

HIS ARMS ARE FULL OF BROKEN THINGS

(After Charlotte Mew, in a poem by Ray Liversidge)

The sun is out in Spring as all things are
but he fiddles listlessly with something unmendable
in the yellow September glare

her heart
or a marriage
or something more complex

the relationship with a daughter perhaps
the endless failures at employment
a social mask for wearing to the garden

party. There are no tears
that you can see and not much more drama
it's not like tv

although he's into singing
he can't seem to strike the right
note

with others on e-harmony.
He wonders why the little dents
and scratches

appear on his car
like parking tickets
in the Spring

and his dreams are full
of money flying out of his pockets
like birds in a seasonal migration

forgetting to return.
He's always preparing to move
but when he looks up from packing
his arms are full of broken things

THE FIRE DOESN'T REMEMBER ANYTHING

What we established while the flakes of light grey ash
Fell against the darker ash colour of the sky was that
Each person's pain while sharing generalities with others
Was particular. Each had a particular smell and colour and feel
Like a jerky camera looking out the back window as an uncle
And nephew staying home to fight the fire
Grew smaller and when the fire had gone
Disappeared altogether. After little dirt road tracks wound down
                the face
There was nothing in the cooling air but brick structures
And the irony always struck me that chimneys
Built to contain fire were sometimes the only thing left
And guilt of course. When I saw each person in session
I would hear their particular confession I was just in a different
                place
For no particular reason; I had gone down to the newsagents to
                get the paper
But then they told me I couldn't go back anymore
Along that road, but I knew they were still waiting for the news
In the paper I had that was not burnt up. The quizzical face
On the blue heeler as I drove away. Someone found him lost and
                scared
On the road and put him in the ute. He didn't understand where
                his men had gone.

When the fire roared over the hill it was a freight train
Forty metres high
And four kilometres long

I had met her about a year after he died, he said
She had an autistic son and now she just said she hadn't finished
            with the dead.
She couldn't do it and now we can just be friends but I can't see
            the boy wanting
To play without getting tears in my eyes. We can't just be friends
            if I can't see him
And just say Goodbye without being like that. She can't take it,
            she said.

And then there's the iron, grey as the ash was with rust brown
            stains around the nailholes
Bleeding out like the house had a life just blown out and the roof
            fallen now onto ash-
Coloured concrete while the tourists starting to come up the road
            from the city
Photographing the bright lime green shoots pushing up through
            dark earth
In the midst of everything dead. It's so unfair she said I can't sleep
Because this all comes back every night I remember
All this but the fire
Is just the fire.
The fire doesn't remember anything

HOLDING THE EGG

When she was eight
she used to go riding
but the parents
wouldn't let her go riding
you can go to the farm they said
but you can't go riding.
Well you know don't you
that she went to the farm
and she rode that horse
and of course she fell off
and of course she broke her arm
and of course she went home
and didn't tell she broke her arm.
She sat down to watch television
until she could feel her mother looking at her
and of course her mother knew she'd been to the farm
and of course she said you rode that horse didn't you
and as the pain ran down her face
she remembered when she was five
she wanted so much to help her mother
while her mother was cooking
and she would beg to help and her mother would say
later I will need this egg
and when she looked down
she noticed
she was holding her arm
in the same way
she held that egg.

A PHOTO OF SOME FISHERMEN IN CORNWALL

Start with the crumpled bruised doona of sky
Triangled to the west out over ocean: the Atlantic
The rock and brown sage green sage hill
Sloping into the estuary.
Move your eye down from the radio mast
To the three boats pulled up on the rock ramp
As if the idea of order existed, here, a long way from Quay West.
Have your eye stopped by the figures of fishermen leaning
                against the boats
So you can tell how cold it's been out on the dull silver water
By the bulk of jumpers under their slicks, the thick boots, the cap
And beanie.
The original white of boats is dirtied from left to right
Until the last little boat bleeds rust down to the ridiculous idea
That it would even survive an ocean.
A large chain the colour of rust perfectly cuts the lower third
Before the causeway of rough granite slabs
Leads us to the dirty white plastic narrative biblical box
Containing dark silver and light silver of fish ends our sight
And we are full.

ALBERT EINSTEIN'S THEORY OF RELATIVITY: GRAVITY
(Under the Milky Way Tonight)

We are falling toward each other
at the speed of space time

        It is mass and density which gives gravity power
        to pull us towards each other
        like the crab nebular
        and the milky way
        speeding toward a collision
        so far away that we forget
        how important it is
        to behave well
        now. How to treat each other in a way
        that balances all those learnt
        things that will disappear.

                Light. Coming out of a morning
                in the country. Grass light green
                and a million shades,
                the mist lifting. I remember
                 the red bridge in
                 Monet's garden.

It is more important than you can ever
imagine. And yet, yes
it will disappear
like everything else. Falling toward
the centre. Memory covers the
territory quickly
so that everything seems like an
illusion. Like a trick of the light

falling toward
all that we have known making
its way through colour
weaving by numbers.
A mass that is mostly air
as all matter is
made of
air. That can be our own galaxy
our own place, but is still
mostly space.

AS THE LIGHT DRAINS AWAY

Outside the light slowly dying
The dying yellow of the end of the day
The air is recently wet
And the ground is washed surface gleaming
Outside the living objects seem to die
As the light fades away from them
Now the yellow electric light has taken over the house
I put away the pieces of the day
And now have to reconstruct the night.

THE DOCTOR WHO TRIED TO TEACH MEN TO SPEAK EMOTION

'The driving forward of desire is a complex end' – William Carlos Williams

You can see him standing there before he goes out on his rounds
to meet them like a figure in an Andrew Wyeth painting he stands
facing his wife and then turns to face the white world in Paterson
with the black of exposed wood in patches sticking through the
snow. As if a camera moves to follow his line of vision through
the slightly rippled imperfect glass you can see the detail of the
pine wood frame of the window. He stamps his feet and moves
out into their world. He works hard in their dark houses. He
works hard long hours each day and has little time to write. He
takes up each precious moment and savours it like a plum. And
as he moves into their rude and broken lives he brings not only
a medicine to ease their bodies but a language to reach into the
bleak perspective and say something about aesthetic.

He knows his time is short. On each farm he must impart the
vision. *No idea but in things* he thinks. Nothing else will reach them
but the objects in their lives. Like a shaman he reaches in and
hauls the diseased parts gleaming out of warmth his hands the
colour of a wheelbarrow.

Once after meagre payment he passes a print of Brueghel's
picture of a dance and the white flash of bums distracts him
through the tunnel of the house. He sees the many pale leggings
shaken out at birth like the walls of a city. Each family's city. His
job is to teach them how to love the taken-for-granted object in
their lives the way he loves her. Stay the violence. Halt the hand
in air. Teach wonder of all that is there. Taste the coldness in the
air.

Sometimes the madness of families is palpable. I still can't sleep
of course. So I hold your absence close to my chest and let
the fan move air over my still face. I used to worry about this
little life of mine and then I'd see a flash of colour or hear an
unmatchable chord and all the worry would be gone with the
water when the rains came in spring. He would leave a sentence
or a phrase with them each visit.

This is just to say he said.

FALLING INTO SLEEP

Falling into sleep now
All the lights are off
I've switched off the electric clock
That used to keep me awake
Rain is staticcing the night

Like a wet radio
That speaks to my blood
Inside a pale covering supported by bone
That speaks to the chlorophyll
In leaves inside the dark

There are other universes
Where we have stayed together
Your little book slips into the world

Under the earth
A moon is moving
As if an ancient civilisation
Dreams it into rising
Every night.

JOY

For me it was walking out on that cold crisp Ballarat morning
While summer was still in bed
Hand in hand with my little daughter. She was three.
She's thirty now and works in a world-famous gallery
In New York. Lives in Brooklyn across that bridge I've never walked
Got the train to BAM. Brooklyn Academy of Music
To see the last performance
Of the Martha Graham Dance Company.

Her hand was puffy with the gift of her mother's DNA
Which would stretch out over years to something
More subtle and slender. The sun
Like a huge theatrical arc light
Yellowing the world as we walked
That dusty road to a fence and a field that contained another being.

A giant slow moving grass mining machine
Pushing its muzzle through the fence
Her hand reaches up to stroke the brown sail
Soft and full as a stretched canvas
The breath coming through cavernous pipes
Like a massive bellows worked by the whole population of the city
          of noise.

COW I say like an idiot and she repeats trusting I will not lead her
          astray
Into that day and the next and the next to the city of now.
I'm sixty-five and know death can't be all that far but still wonder
          how
That old dusty organ of memory can suddenly wake
And crank out enough spark
To send down through the wires
To this moment

CITY OF FALLING ANGELS

THERE IS NO NEED TO TRAVEL TO AMERICA

Just close your eyes
And in three short lines
Your television flickers
Bluely in a corner
Showing endless movies
About sitting in a hotel room
In America watching movies
On television. Stuck in the room
For days on end. Scared to go out
Without knowing where to go out.
On the screen the movie is "Midnight Cowboy"
And the television in the hotel room
Where Jon Voight is stuck is showing
Horrific examples of American television
With characters that make you scared to go out.
So you sit in your room and watch television
Over and over like a late night movie
Which begins with the movie screen within your television
And the sound of cowboys and Indians on television showing you
America like a continual air disaster
Until you can't stand watching any longer
And get up to buy your ticket
For NOT travelling to America
By turning
OFF the television and going out
To find
The blue eyes of television in the streets saying
There is no need to travel to America

PEGGY GUGGENHEIM IN VENICE AND THE UNHEALED SADNESS OVER HER DAUGHTER

Ah Peggy, you had it, that panache, that style
At one of your parties after the war
You re-enact the sinking of the Titanic
Which killed your father. People standing
On the Academia Bridge to watch the dancing
Saw you walk nude into the water of the Grand Canal
And the orchestra following.

After that it never occurred to your daughter that she couldn't do
            anything
But nothing could change the feeling that anything she could do
            wasn't anything.

When I work with young people flirting with hard drugs
Warning: your junkie lover has built up resistance, if you try it, take
half his dose
You didn't listen, you didn't come through that door
Wrapped up against the Tasmanian winter
That rough wool scarf, the gloves
Like your mother you walked nude into the water of the world
The arguments
The weight of words in your hands like water[ii]

Now my favourite doctor says to me
We must meet for coffee in the garden
Of the Peggy Guggenheim Museum
In Venice. Where Peggy lies next to her two
Sleeping dogs, letting them lie, the unhealed sadness
Of the daughter you didn't understand stands next to your ghost

On the dock and breathes a breeze
Through the beech trees
In the garden peaceful as the moon walking nude into water
On the grand canal in Venice
In summer.

TWO PHOTOS OF A MOTHER

I.
In the first you are standing in front of a green field of corn
It could be mistaken for cane from the place where both our
            parents live
But it is not. Your baby sleeps against your chest
Your glasses like a blue tiara forgotten on your head
Your hand reaches out to me which is our secret so far
No-one knows the pleasure we share in each other's company
And even we are moving as if in a dream
Lost in a field the other boys are somewhere
Your smile is reassuring we are safe it says
After travels in a dangerous world
We have found safe harbour or so it seems
On this still day. I wish I had been the father of this child
His hair the colour of mine at his age
In black and white photos with my own mother in a backyard
In Townsville in the fifties. But his actual father,
Biological father, rides a different boat on variable tides
Sometimes high sometimes low but he loves his daddy
You tell me with an exquisite pain in your voice
I am usually paid for hearing. 'No way could it be worse'
As Ray would say of his own daughter in a similar situation.
I don't care. For the moment we have this day, this warm day
In this green field. We may be lost but the baby sleeps on
As if we were all his dream.

II.
In the second you are making statements
Like some kind of constitution of the wronged
Having hired a "professional" your hair is down and beautiful
Your cupped hands cradle your belly about a month before birth
Like the other mothers who have these shots
He's dressed you in white, lace down each arm
And white skimpy pregnant pants
It's like the miraculous, the purity and pregnancy together
This is really a plea you're making to the absent father, come back to me
See what I have done with what we did. My heart goes out to you
I don't know if you know yet that when you went into labour
He went into the door of a holiday place with his new girlfriend
The air was getting cold it must have been a year ago now
The baby just had his birthday. You made a cake
But the wound is so open and current my first impulse is to take you
To the emergency department
As if it is not where you are right now.

WHEN AUTUMN COMES TO BIRDWOOD STREET

The front of my house and street are layered with leaves from oak trees.
So deep the entrance to my drive is hidden and made level.
The sun comes out after three days rain and warms the eyes and feet.
The wind is a stripper and the magic
And loose orange dress
Comes off
When Autumn comes to Birdwood Street.

NOT TOUCHING THE GROUND

When it rains the mother Plover opens her wings
And the babies rush under. At first
I thought they were just sheltering. Now I know
They actually climb up into her body, under the wings
Not touching the ground, until the storm is over.
When she opens her wings and the little chicks
Fall back to earth. The father Plover
Stands a little distance off
Just watching all this.

THE NAME OF THE ROOM

Watching the dusk descend, quotidian
It is leaving the room of the world, you stay
Leaning against me, a Sphinx in Carlton, knees up
With me leaning into you you name the missing colours
Wanting more now, wanting your fair share
I prop up your light body and soul emptied of all that was dark
The soft breeze teasing hair across your face
Thoughts like traffic, crossing the clear place

Across singularity
Across the roofs of the hospital still visible behind us
Across category. Across second opinions
Across the poetry of Pablo Neruda
Across surgery. Across invitation
You come flying

You enter the room called *the woman I love*
To occupy it entirely
To redecorate, to kick your shoes off
And tuck your legs under you
On the white couch reflected in
The polished floorboards
And spend the day looking at the sea
Or absolutely anything else
You want to do, lie on the pier, St Kilda
Under a broiling sun, two little boats
Beached after storm. At peace with the weather of our lives
And waiting for the world to return.

From: TWELVE GACELAS IN MEMORY OF
GARCIA LORCA

GACELA OF YOUNG LOVE SINGING
for Amanda

My heart is broken
It is full of lettuce and celery.
You stood yellow in the big field waving
Like wheat as the train passed
While somewhere in the forest dark thoughts
Fell like a leaf or nut.
Now in the cities smoky juices
I carry round your loss
Like a bag full of oranges
Banging against my empty stomach
And miss your onion warmth
Sorely in the cucumber evenings.

MY MISTAKE: A DIALOGUE

We had spent most of the day moving her stuff
Out of her boyfriend's place in Lyonville, a sleepy
Drive along dusty curves and slopes
Through true Australian bush
Into the near large town

At the end we had set up
And eaten dinner in her new place
A modern flat like many in a suburb like many.
It was hard for me to believe this was progress
Apart from her leaving the man that is.

We had both started work in the same place
On the same day. I had seen her ten years before
Playing netball
Shining.
Next I hear her brushing her teeth in the bathroom.
Then she appears in this red nightie
And kisses me.
It's a good kiss as kisses go.
'Do you want to stay,' she asks very direct
Looking into my eyes.
'That would be good,' I say pretending I knew this was possible
All along. We get into the bed together
We had set up that afternoon and she has put sheets on
She in her red nightie
Me in my jeans and t-shirt.

'Do you want to take your clothes off,' she asks
In a way that says to me this is the expected thing to do.
I take them off in the fading light
My pulse is going now.
I get back into the bed and snuggle my hot body
Up against that red nightie for which I have developed so much
                    affection.
'Not *all* your clothes,' she says.

BAD HOUSE GUESTS

They don't make the bed, but then, that's fair
They didn't sleep in the bed last night, in fact
It was their absence you turned to, very early in the morning.
They don't drive a car up the foggy winter street and park
Where they usually park. You know because you get up
And draw the curtain enough to peek at the quiet blue

Stillness. They don't claim to be ghosts and yet
Who is using the toothpaste in the bathroom
That is not yours; the pink and white deodorant
The second brush, resting on the rippled glass
Of the vanity basin; the crowded shampoo
In the shower. And when you come home

Your cheery greeting echoes down the hall
You can't quite reason for a moment why
Everything is dark and moats float
In the air. But are they parasites? Does she live
Within me now, present, but gone. Like the ghosts
They say they don't want to be they play their part.

Taking a toll like age and surgery
Like cancer and the past these
Bad houseguests of the heart.

THE GOAT WOMAN

There must be something of the believer in such a shepherd.
Her face as full as the moon on nights you can count the colours
                     after dark.
The black gum of her boots suck paddock in her mother-
                     comfort stride.
After rain the dank and rancid waft of urine and wet warm fur
Clouds out dense from the closeted animals.

At night I turn in an endless vision of darkness
She sleeps surrounded by the herd.

Her voice stretches out between tree and post.
Their answer quavers back. Sharp white faces
Quest the air and thinly bleating move in nervous spasms
Like the skinny ghosts of stones across the hill.

THE FISHERMAN

As he opened them
Each was like a silver purse
Lined with red privacy
Of internal affairs.

The child stood silent in the bows
White-faced, watching
Clutched tightly to his chest
A bunch of blue fingers.

Like unloved toys the guts were flung, and landed
On the lumpy darkness of the water in random decoration.

In the early hours that birth and death choose
He cleans another fish
And wipes the blood from his knife
On the soft underbelly
Of the moon.

TODAY

It's one of those clear-skied mornings
when the children run to school
racing the excitement in the river
as it leaps up the mountain
to warm itself
against approaching winter.

LOOK HOMEWARD ANGEL

HOW BIRDS GET LOST: II

They come up shining
And silver over the great curve
Like an unpronounceable and serious
Giant mechanical arm
Of modern mother Russia
Or an American B52
Silent in the jet stream
And arcing
After the sun
Which disappears
Towards Newfoundland
Or Iceland and Norway
In the other direction
Until they hit serious pollution
Somewhere now about the 60th parallel
And creeping northward

Establishing confusion
In the skies over Finland
Or freezing into the lakes of France
The giant birds of Rome
Stuck ungainly
In the most beautiful starvation

Or mistaking the glare
From a car park
For natural water
Plummeting
The body unmarked
Apart from the broken-necked
Death in Texas.

I. WHAT THE TREES SAY

Happiness? He spoke the word.
Are ghosts happy?
Shit I wish the wind
Would sing through these trees.
On a night like this
A game of cards is like a bed
Dragged into the middle of a room
That painting: *Shearers gambling for a bride.*
You hear the sounds?
The normal sounds
After the transfusion.
Emptier than silence. Nothing. Nobody,
The nameless sounds.
The music, a little laughter, a letter.
Everything after is so much dust
And death making his rounds.
All of you who believe
There is no evil
That the world is good
Should go out
On a night like this.
When the axe comes into the forest
The trees say: Look!
The handle is one of us

II. WHAT THE MUSIC SAYS

Before it is light
Before it is light, when you've dressed and gone into the stable
The animals are lying there
Lying there on beech leaves
And your tiredness like a child you have dragged from its sleep
And through the window you see the span of stars
The span of stars into whose well we are thrown at birth
Like salt into water.

Dissolving there like the clear strike of a bell
Through air, over valleys, separated, and yet
Close as the young eye is to air.

The soft sound a hand makes
Moving through air, forming the loving rug of comfort
The dream of waves on the lake. This memory of sound
Is as real as sound itself. We, moving all the time
With knowledge, our inner ear
And a vast range for sound, based only
On a handful of notes.

So; before it is light, the not-quite-light
Evokes the possibility of hope, moving as it does
Out of darkness, out of the home of death
Out of the area where infinite numbers reign supreme

Before it is light; a young child
Moving jerkily across a landscape
At first a move; and then stillness.
He sees his breath become visible
In the coldness of air

That could take his breath away
And yet holds in his mind the knowledge
Of parents still sleeping in the warm breath of their room.

Before it is light
When you've dressed and gone into the stable
And I am feeling foolish on a farm
When the single cow
Has come down to the single bale
With all her cowness and impatience
And I am such a city person now
With such a city softness

The animals are lying there
Waiting for your presence and what that means for them.

Lying there on beech leaves,
And your tiredness like a child you have dragged from its sleep
And our sleep joining together, again, after a long time,
Like the breath of a child.

And through the window you see the span of stars
The notes, breath, moves through the living pipe
Out over the lazy tongue, the way tide, moves in and out
Over estuary sand, snaking into the river, seen high
From above our moment of peace.

The span of stars into whose well
We are thrown at birth
Like salt into water.

Dissolving and clouding, returning
To those elements that first made life
Before there was life. And how poetic;
How romantic now to imagine
Another star with all those elements
Circling in the well. We give ourselves
All our lives these lies
But only be bitter
If we swallow them ourselves
Like the taste of salt in water: that taste
Has so many variations. I hear it now
Singing on the skin in the sweat of our labour
And our love. I hear
That sound in each sound.
So many, into the well, lost
And so much part of each other
So much unrecognised whirling there
Into the well of stars
Before light.

THE RAIN

Everybody argues. They can't stand waiting
For the rain to come.

But the rain has no allegiance.
It doesn't have to come
If it doesn't want to and just the fact
Of everyone waiting like this
Makes it reluctant, slow and luxurious.

I think of you thinking your strong clean thoughts
And how like the rain you are.

The air has rung up the rain
But in the rain's flat the phone just keeps on ringing.
The rain has moved on. Somewhere though the world is wet
And in the space between the wetness
The wires gleam and are singing.

UNSOPHISTICATED POEM WITH HOUND DOG TAYLOR ON THE RECORD PLAYER

The woman of the long night, the moon still
Over shifting clouds above these casual trees
Blue musicians
Taking a break out the back
Way out the back.

The woman who, the dog, stopping on his own agenda,
Trusts.

The woman of ghosts. The woman of white horses.
The woman of all women. The woman of her father.
The woman of dreams. The woman.

The woman of herself. The woman of Indian food.
The woman of taking this no longer. The woman of tea,
Of independence. The woman across the table in the pub.
The woman of knowing.

Thirty miles from town, the white van around the corner
On the dirt road, suddenly, the woman. The woman
Of secret openness. The woman who was loyal
In the face of faces. The survivor.
The woman who's had four men thanks.

This woman. The woman of the blues.
She's the one, I hurt, I love
That woman.

AT A BUS STATION IN CALGARY

When I was young and empty
I did not know I was under-utilised under
pressure under fed every thing went into my mind
undigested and unprotected my mother like
a mother to her chicks
I thought her very words were food I
hung off them like a baby eagle
hanging in the eerie by a thread
of muscle and fibre and bone
I aired my differences
to the max.

When I was young and empty
They poured Christ into my wound
and I could never heal after that
like a thirsty man in the desert
I was always restless
When the teacher
would focus on me I was always the one staring out the window
up the track up that dry and dusty road up that
where the drops of water turned cartwheels of miracles
over and over as the light split them into
an infinity of mind as they fell slow motion into
the air.
And I became a vessel sailing on that air the way
an eagle sails the way
I could not ever sit still the way
I fell tumbling from the nest the way
he said I am
the way.

RAINY AFTERNOON AT DUSK
(A dark little poem)

This light only has the colour of darkness.
Looking out the tinted windows
Of the cafe in Bethesda Hospital
I see only the dark colours
The dark greens
Of the recently wet foliage
The dark yellows of unnamable flowers.

The darkness in the hearts of people
Driving by in the blue-black limousines
The dark navy aggression of the four wheel drives
What darkness have they had to perform to live like this?

Like a cliché the political process
Has reached a dark point in our history
That moment
After the dictator stops smiling
When you realise
It is no longer necessary
To wonder who the secret police are coming for in the night
They are coming for you.

A doctor comes up the steps of the hospital
Hurriedly buttoning his dark suit
What operation is he going to perform?
Outside high up in the El Greco sky
The dark shape of a single bird
I stand to leave
And take my dark presence from the room.

NICHOLAS TEACHES US ABOUT LEAVING

We are the group
Come together to be the group and only by this
Are we the group. This arcane construction of therapy
The circle which began before we existed in it
And will exist after we each leave. In this way
We mirror the wider universe.

Each of us carries our dark package into the room.
Each night we unwrap a little more.
A death here, a separation there
A longing that will never be filled
A vampire's feast of emptiness
Our little victories are entrees
Still the work shines
In its own dull light.

And I am surprised
At what those who I despised
Can teach me.

When Nicholas speaks about his mother
We hear the tightening noose of the old double-bind
Love and dependence. Money and power
Are jealous children peeking through a crack
In the ballroom doors. We squeal at the obvious trap
And touch its shining teeth with a tenderness
That comes from experience
And scars.

He is the one that needs this most I think
As he the one who prepares to go
His baby eyes asked an age-old question
No. I can't tell you what it is
I can only tell you what it felt like – that in dealing
With leaving – wives and lovers mostly
He taught us some nobility, humble
And as close to real as I will ever know.
With each of us he left a gift
His words hang here around the circle like a fire
This ritual in the age of fake ritual.
This coven in the age of computers. He stands to leave
And like the wordless tribe that made us what we are
We ask for messages from the unknown world
We may never know. Tears, quick
Touch us all – and go.

FROM THE MACKSVILLE TO SYDNEY TRAIN

The poem of the landscape flicks by.
Long black logs like the abandoned cigarettes
Of giants. Lonely houses, so I'm not sure
What I saw. A face and hand at the window?
Bleached tin and wood. A black dog stands guard
Over nothing. Desultory Cattle. Windmills
Turn forever like blank roulette wheels:
Everyone's a loser. Gums cluster together
Their burnt history evident as a shared scar.
The occasional flash or black of water.
Off to our right and now left
The alienated highway: its anonymous traffic.
A huge greyness begins to drum on the roof of the train.
A black dog stands guard over nothing.

GACELA OF THE VIETNAM WAR

By the need to be constantly moving
Many loves were found dead in the morning.
Two generations without dancing
Rice paddocks magicked into brown barren basins
The jungle uprooted its leafless trees
And lay dying with its belly to the sky.
Birds crossed the border at night
Leaving a transistor ambush
Doped to its American eyeballs.
The long cool separating barrel of air
Curved down from the bomber to you
And the smell of the burning child running.

COMPASSIONATE

For Steve Biddulph - and My Father

I.

I see the old man sitting there.
We must come together over this.
What is he thinking about? He is thinking about the war
Over and over. And the war has been over
Fifty three years. Fifty three years.
How long has he been sitting there like this?
Fifty three years. How long has he been asleep?
Fifty three years. His life has come and gone
While he has been asleep thinking about the war
Fifty three years. His child has been and gone and come again
Many many times but he has never really seen his child.
His child is writing this
Forty six years. His wife
Where has she been? Sixty years.
I have seen the photos of them
Beautiful young people. Younger than us
Their young faces shining out of the black
And white photos. Fifty three years.
Shining hope. Strong faces. Eaten by the war.
Fifty three years. I see the photo of him with the baby
Taken at the Townsville show. Forty five years.
Where has he been? Fifty three years. He's been in the tunnel,
He's been in the operations room, he's been in the plane.
He's lived in seventeen cities, and not seen them.
He has a granddaughter. Unseen.

II.

My father who saw that plane descend in flames outside of
Ceduna who dragged those burnt and burning bodies out
without thinking about it and now does nothing but think about
it. Those young dead boys from the green fields of Iowa with
nobody they knew or loved around them dying here thousands
of miles from home and nobody but my father did anything
about it and now nobody remembers the graves overgrown in
the hot Australian summer but he remembers he drives three
thousand miles at the age of eighty-four and he cries as he cleans
the graves. Somewhere back in Iowa an old woman looks up
from the TV or a sink with the bright day glaring at her out there
under the Iowa sky and remembers a face.
Nobody but my father held the weight of those light spirits who
flew back to their home in Iowa over the dark and rippling water.
I have flown dark of night 37,000 feet high above dark water
immensity down below; the travellers coming home from LA,
from Disneyland, from whatever it was they were doing with their
lives but my father forgot to do. He sits there now but he was
taken from us as that plane climbed into the sky and then seemed
for a moment to hang still and defying the laws of gravity and
dropped like a stone trying to be a bird for that brief moment
so full of life and the desire to live but dropping out of the sky
onto the dry Ceduna airstrip. That dry grass the spinifex rolling
out to get burnt up by the eating fire that was so eagerly fed that
plane had been so full of fuel. What were they thinking those
young Iowa boys as their lives all ended together there in South
Australia I don't know but I know at least one of them was
thinking no, I don't want to go, not yet, I still have to kiss Bess
she is waiting back on the porch in Iowa or back in the back
seat of my father's Ford and I won't let go and he took over my
father's life and he has been trying to get back to Iowa ever since
and my father shows us the photos of the graves and of the

lonely little funeral and tells us of how the Americans didn't
want to know the Americans who are always so proud of their
boys doing their bit way over there of how my father carried
them into the old aircraft hangar in Ceduna their bodies black
and twisted grotesque little statues of what it was like in hell for
those few seconds that became forever for those boys and for my
father who doesn't see me crying who I never saw cry all my life
who has made this his life which no-one knew about my father
did not tell them what he had been thinking about all these years.
Fifty three years. My father.

THE WEATHER OF OUR LIVES

When you had a shower I thought it was rain.
When you brought all those books home I thought we lived
In a library. When you smiled I suddenly realised
That cliches are based in truth and of course
The day became so much brighter.
When my eyes had rested in yours I could clearly
See for much greater distances, sometimes years ahead
Whereas before I had slowly plodded
From one uneventful day to the next.

Though seasons change over time
Sometimes a storm will spring up on the horizon
And there is nothing I can do to avoid its coming
Batten down the hatches and ride out the worst of it
Hiding in a corner of myself and reading a good book
Until it's over.

Now I am studying hard, becoming
A meteorologist of emotions
So the weather of our lives won't be so
Unpredictable. Each winter I study harder
Gathering in my little room
All the texts of good and bad humor
Until I look up
And the day is running away
Like wild Bukowski horses
Over the hills

But Spring is my favourite season
And it's very hard to keep up
My diligent dedication
To the art of the mind alone.
The body just says 'Leave all that
Alone for a while.' 'Come over here and look at this'
And there you are blooming
Like magnolia or frangipani
Bumped into in the street
Going shopping, riding in from the pool,
Standing in the kitchen
Telling the new drama of your friends' lives
And then I feel I've graduated with a Ph.D. in love
With a special emphasis on the beautiful
Non-conformity of clouds.

CLOSE UP IT MIGHT BE RAIN

For Jean

Close up it might be rain
but at this distance
it's a grey theatrical curtain
with the river and the mountains
performing their ordinary stillness.

She's an Old Testament angel.
Gram would be pleased.
Her garden is her devotion, and
when she plants it rains. It's as simple as that.

Her colours are a palette of years.
At nineteen she rode a yellow motorbike
through dry paddocks and dusty brown roads.
At twenty-seven she begged her rich ex
to buy her a small black and white tv
for the one-year old to watch.
In her thirties and forties a white fluorescent lamp
lit up her studies with three successive boys
to master their autistic focus
into quiet achievement
and the context
of a rounded
centred and fine selfhood.
It sounds easy doesn't it
when you say it like that.

At sixty she sits in a brown recliner
in the green heaven she has planted
above the blue river
and finds it hard to rest.

The river like us rages at its birth
and slow, calmer towards the end
where it empties into
the great ocean.

I love the sound
of her pale grounded feet
padding through the house
the hallway.

When the rain finally arrives
it is a thousand apprentices with
blue rubber hammers
pounding on the roof.

Jean looks out
to the source of the storm. The river
and the mountains
are teaching us acceptance
and stillness.

ATTENTION

Do not leave your longings unattended[iv]
Do not leave your dreams to wander by themselves, guard them
And shepherd them across the hillside in the sunshine
Clouds will come soon enough
And they too
Have their own beauty, curling up into the stratosphere
Where the air is thin and cold
Like water
Bubbling over your hearts of stone to wear them away
To a soft red beating
Which is the essence of us all
Which can recognise
The sound of another similar one
And share a path for a time
We never know how long
But one thing is for sure
Under every footfall
On dark earth and green shoots
It is a precious path.

About The Author

LYNDON WALKER was born in Townsville, North Queensland. He was educated in Psychology at La Trobe University and the University of Melbourne. He graduated with a Masters in Psychoanalytic Studies from Deakin University in 2009. He has taught Psychology at Monash University and The Australian College of Applied Psychology in Melbourne.

Lyndon practised as a Family and Individual Therapist in Melbourne and Launceston before retiring in 2020. He has been published regularly in Australian literary journals over the last thirty years and occasionally overseas. He undertook a world reading tour of London, Paris, New York, Oxford and Princeton in 1994 and in 1996 was awarded the Pablo Neruda Prize for Poetry. He has published five books of poetry and one book of short stories.

He writes poetry, short stories, and academic works on Psychology and Psychoanalysis.

He is the father of one adult daughter and now lives on a green gardened hill overlooking the Tamar River in Beauty Point, Tasmania.

Notes

i Gayelene Carbis, "The Weight of Words in Our Hands Like Water," in *Anecdotal Evidence* (Five Islands Press, 2017).

ii Gayelene Carbis, "The Weight of Words in Our Hands Like Water."

iii After a line in poem by Galway Kinnell, "The Still Time."

iv Line taken from Meme on Facebook, September 2023.

"The weight of words in our hands" from a poem with this title by Lyndon Walker in *Makar Poetry Magazine*, No 14 Vol 2. 1980, following a workshop with Galway Kinnell in Sydney in 1975.